D1784223

MONSTROUS ENCOUNTERS: KRAMPUS

MONSTER EROTICA COLLECTION

SEDUCTIVE CREATURES
BOOK FIVE

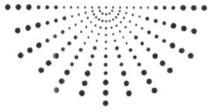

LEE RILEY

* * *

* * *

 Created with Vellum

KRAMPUS BRINGS HIS ROD

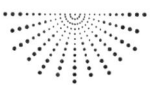

* * *

"Lilibet? Lilibet! LILIBET! What are you doing? Are you on that damn phone again? Have you put up the goats? There's snow on the forecast tonight; they'll freeze. Please, Lilibet, put the phone down and finish your chores."

"Ugh," Lilibet groaned and rolled over onto her back on her queen-sized, angora-covered bed. "Mama can't you do it? I'm in the middle of something. I don't have time."

"What are you in the middle of?" Lilibet's mother Agnes furrowed her brows, not bothering to hide the skepticism in her voice. "Are you taking pictures of yourself?"

"No," Lilibet lied. She had, in fact, been taking pictures of herself.

"Why are you all dressed up?"

"I don't know what you mean."

Lilibet concentrated on her phone, hoping that her mother would go away. She was such a nag, really, she could just as well have brought the goats in to the barn herself. In fact, if she had just done it herself it would have been done by now and everyone's life would have been easier.

"Lili, I hope you haven't forgotten…"

"Forgotten what, Mama?" Lilibet snapped in exasperation, eager to get back to the important matters going on on her phone at that very moment. Her mother was no doubt about to bring up some other boring thing she wanted to do, or rather some boring thing she wanted Lili to do. And she couldn't just state what stupid, pointless task she wanted completed at that very second; she had to go for the passive-aggressive 'HoPe yOu haVEn'T ForGOtteN…'

It was maddening, really, how needy her mother was. How needy both of her parents were. They couldn't do anything by themselves, they were always asking her to take in their goats or clean her room or get her books off the kitchen table or God only knew what else. She had no idea how they were going to survive when she went to Uni the next year.

"It's Krampusnacht," her mother gave her a sly grin and smacked her on the ass. "Naughty little girls who don't do their chores get punished."

"Mama," Lilibet finally cracked a smile, "I'm not a child. I'm going to Uni next year! Besides," she gave her mother a sly grin of her own, "maybe I want to get spanked."

"Lilibet!" her mother erupted in a conspiratorial burst of giggles. "You don't mean that. You're still my little girl, albeit my naughty little girl. Bring in the goats and quit sending dirty pictures to your boyfriend."

"Mama!" Lili pretended to be scandalized, though that was exactly what she had been doing. Well, not exactly-exactly. Technically Stephan wasn't her boyfriend. Technically speaking, she had never met him in person. He lived over two hundred kilometers away and Lilibet still hadn't passed her driver's exam so she hadn't been able to go see him, so they were still Snapchat friends only. Still. Things had looked promising with him, or rather A Thing had looked promising ON him and Lili didn't feel like being interrupted. As usual, her mother had intruded at the worst time possible, but Lilibet knew that there was only one way to get rid of her when she got into one of her moods like this.

She had to pretend to cooperate.

She slid the camera app on her phone closed and looked up at her mother. Mama had probably been very pretty once, Lilibet could tell. She still had rosy cheeks and blonde curls, but her body had become soft with age. And not the sexy kind of soft, like an old-fashioned pin-up; no, just the marshmallow kind. She looked just like all the other Mamas in her village. It was a sad fact, Lilibet already knew, that one day she'd probably suffer the same fate as her mother. She'd marry a local boy and pop out a couple of fat babies and then slowly but surely evolve into a farmwife.

But that day hadn't arrived just yet. For the time being, Lilibet's skin was creamy and her body was tight. She knew very well that her youth wouldn't last forever and she wasn't about to let it pass her by without having a little bit of fun. Surely her mother would understand her desire to create a few wicked memories to look back on fondly when she herself was a farm wife, just like every other woman in their village.

"Well?" her mother kept prodding, refusing to accept the fact that she was just going to have to deal with the animals herself.

"Fine," Lili conceded with a pout on her lips. "I'll bring them in. In a minute."

"Well," her mother looked her over, like she was trying to assess the likelihood that Lilibet would actually do her chores against the frustration of trying to prod her into any kind of work, "okay. Just bring them in please, so they don't freeze."

Lili could tell that her mother wasn't going to let this go entirely but at least she had temporarily given up. Good. She just needed some privacy to put together her look, and anything that would get her mother out of her hair was a win as far as she was concerned, even if it was a short-term win. She'd deal with her mother later.

are you ready?

Lili nearly dropped her phone as it buzzed with excitement.

Contrary to her mother's belief, Lili hadn't forgotten what night it was. Not at all. That was because she'd been preparing for this night for at least a month, choosing her makeup and her outfit and discussing strategy with her girlfriends. It was Krampusnacht, and that meant that every guy in the mountains would be at tonight's bonfire. It was going to be the party of the year, maybe the party of her lifetime depending upon how well things went, and she wouldn't miss it for the world.

> I'm not even dressed yet

She wrinkled her small nose and texted her best friend back, along with a cringe-face emoji:

> my mother is out of control

Lilibet waited as the three little dots appeared on her screen, indicating that Heidi was writing her reply.

> mine is the same
>
> she keeps making up more pointless chores for me to do
>
> I think she knows about the party

Of course both of their mothers knew about the Krampusnacht bonfire. Every person within two hundred and fifty kilometers knew about the party. It was a local tradition that dated back for as long as anyone could remember and Lili had no doubt that both her parents and Heidi's parents had attended the fire before they got old and boring. The only people who didn't attend were the religious fanatics, and even some of them sometimes made an appearance. Especially the men, since they could attend in disguise, have their sanctimonious cake and eat it too.

There wasn't much to do around Lili's village. There wasn't much to do around any of the local villages, aside from drink and fuck, which every local unmarried person did with great vigor. A party like tonight's fire was a once-per-year opportunity to create once-in-a-lifetime experiences.

How much time do you need?

Lilibet texted her best friend, trying to plan their escape perfectly. Heidi was the only one of her friends who had her license and was thus the designated driver for their squad, though she didn't have her own car. Not a single one of the girls had permission to be out that night so they'd come up with an elaborate master plan to pick everyone up: behind barns, around corners, down the block... anywhere where they could slip from their parents' watchful gazes.

thirty minutes

Heidi texted back,

be ready out by Rosa's place, I'm
going to pick you both up at the
same time

Lilibet agreed and got to work. She needed fifteen minutes to get to Rosa's, including the time it would take to get out of her own house, so that gave her only fifteen to finish putting on her face.

Perfect. She cracked open the plastic box that held some of her most prized possessions: her makeup collection.

Lili gave herself a brief glance in the mirror, but didn't need to study her reflection because she already had a plan in mind. This event called for a dramatic look. The night was cold, it was dark out, and the bonfire was held in a forest which didn't have much light even during the day. She expected a lot of dark shadows and flickering lights. Lili dabbed gold glitter onto her eyelids and cheekbones and then lined her eyes heavily with black coal. Funny that coal was what was used to threaten naughty children; she'd love to receive this eyeliner as a gift. It was expensive, though, and her father thought that it made her look too mature, which was stupid because he was also constantly complaining about how immature she was.

Next she went for a deep red lip in matte velvet, for a festive, Christmassy look. She topped this with a bee sting cream that was supposed to make her look like she had lip injections. It didn't look like real lip injections, of course, if people could achieve that for ten bucks they'd never pay for real ones, but it wasn't that bad either. She puckered her lips and admired herself in the mirror. She added a little drop of gold highlight over her Cupid's bow and blew herself a kiss.

Lili had achieved just the look she was going for. The black eyeliner made her look sultry and sophisticated but the red lip and glitter gave her look some holiday cheer, plus it would look amazing reflecting in the fire. She loved it and it matched her outfit perfectly.

It hadn't been easy to choose an outfit for the night. Looking sexy outdoors while it snowed was an art form, but it was one that Lilibet and her friends had perfected growing up in the mountains. Her furry boots had been an obvious choice, of course. They looked cute and they were the warmest things she'd owned. She'd matched these with a snowflake-dotted wool sweater topped by a fitted, hunter green, down-lined parka, and a rich burgundy corduroy mini-skirt. She was going to top everything off with a camel colored cashmere hat and scarf set that she had stolen from her mother's closet and planned to return, her mother none the wiser.

The real piece de resistance, however, had been the wool thigh-high stockings. They looked like regular tights under her skirt, but if she bent over just right whoever was lucky enough to get a view would see that she was wearing nothing but a red silk thong underneath. It was the ideal choice for the night with its very… particular festivities and traditions.

She turned around and bent over in front of the mirror, checking the cheekiest detail of her look. She's shaved and rubbed cream into her skin that afternoon and the swells of her ass looked just like a ripe, creamy peach. The ruby red slip of her panties was just bright enough to stand out against her burgundy skirt and her body flushed with naughty anticipation of the night's pleasures.

Lili checked her phone. It had only taken her ten minutes to get her makeup on point. That meant that she still had five minutes. She glanced at the box labeled 'old photos' up on her wardrobe and wondered if she had time.

She would if she was quick.

Lili scampered across the room and pulled the box down silently, removing a slender purple vibrator that she'd bought secretly in a sex shop on a class trip to Vienna the past year. She gave it a shake and slid the on button to the highest vibration, knowing that she didn't really have time to warm herself up.

She didn't even pull her panties to the side, and the vibration would have been too intense for direct contact anyways. The gently pointed tip of the device slid up and down the silk crotch of her panties, bringing about an immediate response in her body.

If only the real boys she'd been with had this function, Lili suppressed a giggle, not wanting to alert her parents. Then it would be no wonder why everyone was in such a hurry to lock one down with marriage.

It didn't even take her the full five minutes. A series of snapshots of moments floated through her mind as the vibrator worked it's magic, a kiss here, a finger there… it wasn't long before Lili was holding her breath, struggling to stay quiet as her body shook.

Perfect timing. She hid her toy back in its special spot and made her way to the back door.

"Lili?" she heard her mother's voice call to her from the front room. "Are you bringing those goats in?"

"Yes, Mama," she yelled, slamming the door behind her before her mother could continue her line of questioning.

She stepped out the door and briefly glanced at the goats. Shit. They were all huddling in the far corner of their pasture, all the way on the other side from the barn door. If they had any brains at all, they would have just walked into the warm barn when she opened the door for them. Unfortunately, she knew these goats too well. They never just walked into the barn for the night, they always had to be chased in, one by one.

She didn't have time to actually herd them in now, she'd forgotten all about them when she spent her extra five minutes playing with herself, and all she had to show for her troubles now were wet panties.

"Sorry guys," she apologized as she hopped over the fence and across the pasture. She'd have to just bring them in when she got home later, hopefully they'd be okay out there for a few hours. That's what their fur was for anyway, and Lili knew just how warm it was her mother had used it to make the blanket on her bed. They'd probably be fine.

It was already getting colder out. The wind whipped Lili's nose so she pulled up her mother's scarf as she made her way through the trees on the shortcut to Rosa's place. There wasn't any snow on the ground yet, but there surely would be by the time the party was over. Maybe sooner. The chill in the air was nipping at her and making her eyes water.

Lilibet slid through the tall pines expertly, like she knew them like the back of her hand, because she did. She'd been taking the same shortcut to her friend's place since she was in kindergarten. The forest was a second home to her and she loved it, spooky as it was.

"Rosa? Rosa!" Lilibet hissed under her friend's window. She crouched down and strained her ears, trying to hear whether Rosa was alone in there.

Her friend's parents were even more strict than hers, and Lili knew that Rosa's father still spanked her, and not in the playful way that she expected to be spanked later that night. She was very brave, sneaking out like this, and Lili admired her.

The window unlatched and slid down slowly, and Lili saw her friend's face in the dark.

"Help me out," Rosa stretched one denim-clad leg through her window.

"Is this what you're wearing?" Lili asked, then immediately regretted the question. Rosa's parents were so strict that it wouldn't surprise Lili at all if this was the sexiest thing she owned. "You look amazing!" she immediately followed up before Rosa could answer her. "Those jeans fit you perfect."

"Thanks," Rosa smiled. "I was worried if I looked okay but I don't really have anything else. Anyhow, come on, we have to hurry so that Heidi isn't waiting for us."

Rosa slid the rest of the way out of the window and Lilibet helped her to slowly slide it closed so that the chill air didn't attract Rosa's parents' attention. The night was electric with energy. Both girls were practically shaking with excitement as they hid inside the old bus shelter near Rosa's house and waited for their ride. Lili stared up the street, past all the houses twinkling with their Christmas lights, willing the van to appear.

"I can't believe that Markus let Heidi take his van," Rosa mused quietly.

Lilibet couldn't believe it either. Markus was Heidi's dorky older brother. He was home for the holidays from Uni, where he had been studying architecture. He was nothing like the guys Lili was interested, neither in looks or character. Markus was a real know-it-all and he looked like the stereotypical uptight nerd with his stupid glasses and pale, skinny body. Usually he never did anything nice for Heidi, not for free at least, and Lili had also been shocked when Heidi had said that he was cooperating that night. They had previously assumed that Heidi would have to steal the van. It wouldn't have been the first time.

"Is that them?" Rosa asked, leaning forward on her seat.

It was. Markus' old white van puttered around the corner and pulled up to a stop in front of them. The passenger door swung open and the girls were immediately met with Heidi's apologetic expression.

"I swear to God he said that we could borrow the fan," she immediately explained.

Markus leaned over his sister from the driver's seat "And you lucky girls are getting a chauffeur with it! But it's not going to be free."

"Oh my God, come on Markus, don't be like this," Lilibet whined. He was such a dickhead, honestly. "We don't even have that much money. Only enough to get drinks. Come on…"

"Well I didn't say that it would cost you any money," Markus intimated.

"What? What is that even supposed to mean?" Rosa cringed.

"Just get in the van," Heidi groaned back, "before this thing wakes your parents and the rest of the village up."

Lilibet swung the back door open and Rosa climbed in ahead of her. She took her place and Markus was already peeling off before she got the door shut.

"Three down, two more sluts to go," Markus chirped from the driver's seat as he rumbled along.

"Shut up, asshole," his sister hit him in the arm.

"Hey now," he laughed, I can just dump the three of you out on the street right here, if that's what you prefer. I can go to Krampusnacht alone, see who else wants a ride." He tapped a plastic Krampus mask he had hanging from his rear view mirror. "And don't forget," he added, grinning in the mirror, "there's still the matter of my payment."

"No one is going to pay you, loser," his sister insisted, crossing her arms over her chest.

The van screeched to a halt.

"Fine," he replied, his voice smug. "You girls can walk."

"What?" Heidi demanded. "No!"

"Then you have to pay up. Or rather, you two have to pay up," he turned around in the mirror to stare at his backseat passengers.

"We told you," Lilibet furrowed her brows. "We hardly have any money."

"I don't want money."

"What do you want?"

"One of you has to suck my dick."

There was a moment of silence before all three girls burst out laughing.

"I meant one of you two," Markus groaned, as though that was the only part of his demand that the girls might have found objectionable.

"Why are you so gross?" Heidi demanded. "This is why you don't have any friends."

"I don't need any friends," Markus countered, "look what good yours are doing for you. They can't even give one single, teensy tiny blow job so that you can all go to your party."

"Well if it really is that tiny..." Lilibet couldn't help herself but to tease him. Markus had provided her that set up and there was no way she was going to pass on that opportunity to ridicule him. Especially given his current behavior.

"So that's a yes?" Markus ignored the joke while the other girls laughed.

"No it's not a yes, Dumbass," Lili laughed. "If we were willing to suck someone's dick for a lift, we would have asked someone with a cooler ride."

The girls could tell by the expression on Markus' face that the point had landed.

"Okay," he drawled, "then show me your pussies."

"I'm telling Papa," Heidi interrupted.

"Go right ahead," her brother sneered, "you think he's going to be happy about you sneaking out to attend tonight's little fuckfest with your slutty friends? Every single one of you is going to be grounded until you're fifty."

"Yeah," Heidi growled back, "Papa is going to be pretty upset when he finds out that you were going to deliver me to that fuckfest after assaulting his friends' teenaged daughters."

"Fine," Markus spit out. "I'm not driving you for free though. You have to pay for my drinks. Also," he looked in the backseat again, "you two have to kiss."

"Fine," Lilibet interrupted before Heidi could keep arguing with her brother. She leaned over and quickly kissed Rosa on her pink lips. "There. We kissed. Let's go."

"Not like that," Markus replied, his voice dripping with mocking contempt. "You have to give her a real kiss. With tongue."

Lili didn't want to argue with Markus all night. They still had to pick up Kristina and Lana, plus they had to stop at the grocery store to buy liquor.

"Fine," she spat back, and before Rosa could protest — she was a bit of a prude — Lili was plunging her tongue into her friend's mouth.

Rosa whimpered in response but she didn't push Lili away or even close her mouth. Instead her tongue met Lili's and the girls kissed, tentatively at first but then with more passion.

It was different from kissing a boy, Lilibet observed. Usually, when a boy kissed her, he was pushing his big, slobbery tongue into her mouth. Rosa's tongue was small and she tasted like the marzipan candies she had been eating earlier in the evening. She was sweet and soft, and it was easy for Lili to see why men and even other women would prefer this over the clumsy kisses given by men.

"So are you two lesbos now or what?" Heidi interrupted, causing Rosa to pull back and end the kiss. "There," she turned to her brother, "you got your little show. Can we go now?"

Apparently that kiss had been enough to satisfy Markus because he put the van in gear and continued to putter around the village, picking up Lana first and then poor Kristina who had been waiting out in the cold for nearly an hour.

"Sorry," Heidi apologized as the last girl slid into the backseat next to Lilibet, "my brother was extorting us."

Lili and her friends weren't about to let Markus put a damper on their evening. He took them to the grocery store where they stocked up on vodka, premade egg nog, hard seltzers, and even a few bottles of Prosecco.

As the girls made their selections, Lili wandered up and down the aisles, admiring all of the Christmas goodies on display. The shelves were fully stocked with stollen, candied nuts, and all the other treats that appeared every year when the weather got cold.

She was tempted by a chocolate orange when a deep voice gave her a startle.

"Those are only for good girls."

Lili dropped the orange and bent over to pick it up but quickly stopped herself, remembering the features and limitations of her current outfit. She knelt down to pick up the orange instead and by the time she glanced up at whoever had spoken to her, he was already rounding the corner to the next aisle and all she could see was his big frame, dressed all in black, and the back of his black hair. She hadn't even heard anyone walking behind her until he had spoken up.

Weird.

She placed the orange back on the shelf and hurried off to find her friends, who were already queuing with their selections.

By the time the van chugged its way up the mountain to the trailhead, all of the good parking was already occupied and Markus had to head up to the next trailhead to find a space, which meant that he and the girls would need to hike through the woods for a good thirty minutes before they reached the fire, which they could hear and smell long before they could see.

The cold wind nipped at Lilibet's cheeks, both the ones on her face and her ass, but her skin was electric with excitement. She before they even reached the party her nostrils had filled with the scent of burning pine.

"Here," Heidi handed her an open bottle of vodka. "Take a swig of this so you don't freeze."

Lili took a long pull from the bottle and wrinkled her nose as the burning liquid slipped down her throat. She hadn't eaten much of the supper her mother had prepared, a goulasch which was usually one of her favorites, she had just been too excited. Now she was regretting her empty stomach.

The trail broke into a clearing and the girls were met with a towering bonfire surrounded by girls in the most revealing winter wear possible and boys wearing Krampus costumes of varying effort and quality.

Some of them, like Markus, just had horned plastic devil masks. Lili recognized several boys from her class immediately, standing around drinking or chasing girls with their birch rods. Some of the other guys had much more elaborate costumes though, including fur pants and handmade paper maché masks with real animal horns.

One man was even shirtless.

Lili spotted him from across the fire and it was like her eyes were magnets, she had no power to tear them away.

Who the hell was that?

Who in her village was built like that?

No one that she could think of. Or maybe one of the married men secretly had a six pack under his sweater? He wasn't wearing a ring. He wasn't wearing much of anything at all, despite the freezing weather, just black trousers and an elaborate horned mask. A birch switch hung from the belt loop of his pants and Lilibet couldn't see his face at all, it was completely obscured by his mask, which resembled a large animal skull with big black holes for eyes and nostrils.

She had to talk to him.

Lili unscrewed the lid on her egg nog and took a swig to steel her courage, then made her way around the fire, through the throngs of youths. She hadn't made it halfway around before someone gave her a swat on the butt, over her skirt.

"Have you been a naughty little girl?" a boy her own age wearing a goat mask asked.

"Laurent, you're a dog, not a goat," Lili laughed back.

"You want to see my tail?"

"I don't know, how long is it?"

"Come look."

"I just got here," Lilibet protested. She'd always liked Laurent, he was cute in a boyish way with his curly hair and his contagious smile.

"Then maybe you'd like one of these?"

Laurent held his palm open. There, lying dead in the center, was a small blue tab.

"MDMA?"

"Yeah. Go ahead."

Lili took the pill and swallowed it with another swig of eggnog. It went right down and she knew that she'd be feeling good in twenty minutes or so.

"Now there's the matter of your payment," she teased, tickling Laurent's chin under his mask.

"You don't have to pay."

"Oh, I want to. Come over here where we can have some privacy."

Lilibet led Laurent away from the fire where they could be alone behind a large pine, but not so far away that they no longer enjoyed the fire's heat.

"I don't have any more money," she pouted, putting her finger up to her lips like she was thinking hard.

"Uh oh," Laurent pressed her back against the tree and pulled his mask up. "How are you going to pay?"

"Is there something else I have that you might want," Lili grinned, wiggling her butt against the tree. Laurent's body was pressed against hers now and he pressed his lips to hers, taking his time kissing her, tasting the eggnog on her.

"Let me see," his fingers traveled up her sweater, the cold causing her to jump and let out a squeal. He found her bra and pulled it down so he could play with her nipple. The cold gave Lili a jolt and she clung tighter to him, taking in his scent, soap and beer.

"What else have you got," he murmured into her neck. His hand slid out of her sweater and up her skirt this time, and now it was his turn to be surprised. "You are a naughty girl," he grinned. "Aren't you freezing?"

"Warm me up," Lilibet purred back. Laurent responded by fingering the soft silk fo Lili's panties with his now-warm fingers.

"I think you might have something here that interests me," Laurent teased, stroking Lili gently.

She was already feeling the effects of that tab she took, thanks to her empty stomach and the liquor. She spread her thighs slightly to allow Laurent to slide his fingers into her panties, where he already found her wet.

"Is there somewhere we can go?" she sighed, feeling his erection straining through his pants and rubbing her leg.

"Umm," Laurent picked up his head and looked around for a moment, "my car? I parked at the trailhead. The close one."

Lilibet nodded in response. It was only a five minute walk or so. She grabbed his hand and let him lead her through the crowds of partiers just arriving.

"It's over here," he led her to a mid-sized sedan. "You want to get in the back?"

Lili didn't care that other people were staring at them. Who were they to judge? They'd probably be doing the same thing in a few hours' time. She waited for Laurent to unlock his car and then climbed in in front of him on her hands and knees.

She heard the car door shut and didn't even have time to turn around before Laurent had her skirt pulled up to her hips.

"You look so sexy, Lili," he purred, burying his face in her cunt. "Let me taste you."

He pulled her panties to the side and licked her, up the length of her wet lips, lingering on her hard clit. He pushed a finger inside of her, first one, then two, then fucked her gently while still eating her out.

"Do you have a condom?" Lili asked breathlessly. "I'm not on anything…"

"Yeah," Laurent popped open the glove compartment and rifled around for a moment before locating a small plastic package.

Lili stayed on her hands and knees while she heard him rip it open and fumble with it. It wasn't long before she could feel his smooth head rubbing up and down her sensitive skin.

"You want it?" he asked her, his voice soft but firm.

"Yes, Laurent, give it to me."

Lili was eager for Laurent's cock but she was also eager to get back to the party. The night was young and she had a lot of fun in store. She didn't want to spend the entire evening in the backseat of Laurent's car with him.

He didn't make her beg for it. Laurent slid his cock into her warm pussy, first just the tip, then further and further in until he was filling her up. Lilibet braced herself, placing one sweating palm against the fogged up window and jumping when someone walking by hit the window back from the other side. She heard Laurent laugh softly as he picked up his pace, fucking her quickly but gently.

His breath caught in his throat and Lili's brow wrinkled. Was that it? She hadn't finished. She hadn't even come close.

To her disappointment, though, Laurent was already pulling out and removing the now-filled condom.

"Thanks Lilibet," he huffed, giving her a friendly slap on the ass. "That was great."

"Sure…" Lili stared out the window, adjusting her skirt.

"I'm going to head back to the fire. Can you make sure that the car is locked when you leave?"

"What?" Lili was caught off guard. They weren't returning to the party together? That was fine, she guessed, after that performance she was no longer interested in Laurent anyways. "Sure, I'll lock up."

Laurent left her alone for a moment. Oh well, she thought to herself. It hadn't been the first time one of her classmates had been completely clueless when it came to getting women off. She smoothed out her outfit and got out of the car.

It was no longer crowded like it had been earlier. In fact, Lili was alone amongst the haphazardly parked vehicles. The empty parking lot was giving her the creeps and she was in a hurry to return to the fire with her friends.

"What's the matter, little girl?" a familiar voice said from behind her.

Lilibet spun on her heel and found herself face to face with the shirtless man she'd spotted from across the fire earlier. Up close he was even hotter, much bigger than her, well over two meters. His chest was broad and well muscled and he smelled like smoke and coal, like he'd just ascended from hell.

"That kid not man enough for you?" the man asked, chuckling quietly.

"Oh, Laurent?" Lili tried to act casual. "No, it's not like that. We're just friends."

"Just friends?" the man tossed his masked head back. "You let all your friends fuck you and then leave you like that? No wonder you're on my list."

It had begun to snow softly and Lilibet licked a few flakes from her lips. "I don't know who you are," she muttered back. This guy was creepy, albeit in a hot way. She didn't know if she wanted to run from him or throw herself at him.

"Sure you do," he replied quietly, grasping her by her upper arm. "Tonight's my night."

Oh. This guy was going to go all the way with his Krampus schtick. Okay, that was fine. Lili smiled and looked closer at his mask.

"Is that real bone?" she reached out and touched it and was surprised to find, first, that it was real bone, and second, that it was warm.

Without thinking, her fingers drifted from the bone mask down to the man's chest. They traced the dips and swells and Lilibet could feel herself getting wet and tingly again. "I need to get back to the fire," she said quietly, not making any move to actually leave.

"You've been a very, very bad girl, Lilibet," the man replied.

"How do you know my name?"

It must have been someone she knew but she had no idea who it could be.

"Oh I know all about you. I know what you've done. I know what you want to do." The man — Krampus — stepped closer and wrapped his arm around Lilibet's waist. "You don't want to go back to that fire."

Lili didn't reply. She wanted to see Krampus' face. He was right, though, she didn't feel like going back to the party.

"Let's get out of here."

"What's your name?"

"Krampus."

Okay. Fine. He didn't want to say. That was alright, it was even kind of hot. Lili knew that she wasn't really taking any sensible precautions, but it was hard to behave sensibly when this guy was so sexy and she had never heard of any kind of violent crime happening with a stranger where she lived. Her only real fear was that this guy was married, his wife would find out what she was about to do, then the whole village would think she was a whore.

"Holy shit," Krampus led Lili to a shiny black motorcycle, "is this yours?"

"Yes. Put this on." He handed her a helmet and she obeyed immediately. Lili had never been on a motorcycle before and it was something she'd always wanted to try.

Krampus got onto the bike and Lili climbed on behind him, wrapping her arms and legs around him, holding on tight for safety. She could barely get her arms around his tree trunk chest.

The bike pulled out of the parking area and tore down the mountain, hugging curves and growling through tunnels and covered bridges. Lili gripped Krampus between her thighs and scooted her butt forward, partly because she wanted to touch him and partly because the way he drove scared her.

They sped through the forest and then past the town's twinkling Christmas lights, some of which had already been turned off for the night. Snow fell softly and they were the only people on the road.

"Where are we going?" Lili yelled when things began to look a little bit too familiar, but Krampus didn't respond, either because he couldn't hear her or because he didn't care.

Soon enough Lilibet's suspicions were confirmed.

"Why are we back at my house," she whined, now worried that Krampus was actually one of her father's stupid friends who was just ruining her night. The motorcycle pulled up beside the barn and the engine died.

Krampus put his finger over his mask in the 'shush' gesture, picked up Lili, and threw her over his shoulder like a sack of potatoes.

"Hey," she hissed quietly. She didn't know what he was up to but she also didn't want to alert her parents.

Krampus carried Lilibet to the pasture and dumped her on her butt in the snow.

"Hey what do you think you're doing?" she demanded, but he only responded by gesturing toward the pasture with a finger tipped in a long, pointed black nail that looked like a claw.

Weird. Was that part of his costume? Lili glanced where he was indicating.

"Fuck! Shit! God damn it," she scrambled to her feet and ran to open the barn door. She'd forgotten all about the goats and now they were huddled in a corner shivering.

"Come on! Come on Basti, come on Ginger!" she called them and most of them proceeded into the barn. "Shit!" Lili exclaimed when she saw that one of the little black and white ones was on the ground. She raced over to him and picked him up in her arms, trying to rub him awake.

Krampus joined Lilibet in the pasture and took the goat from her arms.

"Is he dead?" she asked, feeling genuinely remorseful. She didn't like her chores but she did care for the goats.

"Not yet," Krampus answered.

"Can you help him?" Lili demanded, following Krampus as he carried the little goat into the barn.

"I can save him, but you're going to have to pay for what you've done."

"Fine. I don't have any cash —"

"You know that's not what I meant," Krampus teased.

Lilibet looked him up and down. "Can you really save him?"

Krampus nodded.

"Okay fine. Do it."

She watched in awe as Krampus was able to revive the little goat, rubbing his back with his black claws.

It only took a few moments before the goat was scampering back to his mother.

"Well if that's all it took—" she started to complain but Krampus stopped her, putting his hand over her mouth.

He spun her around and pushed her over a couple bales of hay so that she was bent over in front of him, exposed.

"Hey!" she protested.

In response he hooked one of his claws around her panties and pulled them to her knees.

"What are you doing?" Lilibet demanded, looking over her shoulder. She tried to jolt upright when she saw him draw his birch switch from his belt but he pushed her back down on her stomach.

"I told you that you were going to have to pay for what you've done, Lilibet," Krampus growled. "You've been a brat all year, you tease the boys in your class and you don't mind your parents, you nearly just killed that goat. It's time for you to learn what happens to such naughty little girls."

This was kinky.

"So you're going to spank me?" Lili purred, assuming that Krampus would give her a few warm up smacks before giving her what she really wanted.

"I'm going to punish you. And you're not going to like it. Put this apple in your mouth so that no one hears you," he tossed her an apple from the bin beside him, "and place your hands palm side down beside your shoulders. Turn your toes in toward each other."

Lili followed Krampus' instructions, turning her toes in so that her vulva was exposed as well as her ass. She'd never done anything like this before. It was scary but it was also exciting.

Any misconceptions that Lilibet had about how this was all just play were immediately cleared up with the first thwap from Krampus' birch. Lili jumped and squealed like a piglet as her ass cheeks burned.

He'd struck her like he meant to punish her. She removed the apple from her mouth to complain but before she could get a word out he'd struck her again, this time on the backs of her thighs.

"Hey what the hell do you think—" he struck her again, this time striking her vulva. Lilibet could feel the tears welling in her eyes.

"You've got to learn, Lilibet. And get back into position or I'll start all over again. You don't want that do you?"

He struck her twice more and Lili immediately obeyed and bent over for him, apple in her mouth.

"Point your toes. You're clenching so that it doesn't hurt as bad."

Lilibet could already feel her legs trembling. She couldn't bring herself to pigeon her toes again.

"Fine," Krampus laughed. "If you want to do this the hard way…"

This time he helped himself to a large piece of ginger from the root bin. Lili watched from the corner of her eye as he scraped the peel off with his claw and she wondered what he was going to do with the peeled piece he had left. Make her eat it?

Without warning, Krampus spit on the piece of ginger and then rubbed his saliva over the surface. He pushed Lili down harder on her stomach, holding her still with one hand while he used the other to insert a knob of the peeled ginger into her clenched asshole.

Lili whimpered again, then immediately unclenched to relieve the burning feeling inside of her now. As soon as she unclenched, Krampus was at it again, spanking her mercilessly for her bratty behavior.

She wanted to beg him for forgiveness, to promise that she'd never skip her chores again and that she'd obey her parents forever, but she was gagged with the apple. Her skin was on fire, her thighs, her ass, and her face were burning.

"Are you going to be a good girl now?" Krampus asked, his voice still calm.

Lilibet nodded vigorously.

Krampus reached a finger down and stroked Lili's bare vulva. "Do you promise?"

Lili involuntarily leaned back into his touch and nodded again she started to get up but he pushed her back down with one hand while he worked the fly of his pants with the other hand.

"If you promise to be a very, very good girl from now on I'll let you have what you want."

Lilibet's eyes bulged as Krampus pulled his other rod from his pants. It was long and thick, maybe the nicest cock she'd ever seen in her life. She couldn't wait to feel it inside of her, but instead of filling her tight hole he started by teasing her with it, rubbing the head up and down her vulva.

Her body clenched and then relaxed immediately as the ginger still inside of her burned. She wanted

Krampus so bad now and she couldn't even take the smallest step to relieve her own desire because of that damned ginger. Lili whimpered and wiggled her ass in front of Krampus.

"Okay. I can see that you're going to behave now. This might hurt a little bit…"

Krampus inserted the tip of his cock into Lili's burning slit. Her skin was so sensitive now after the spanking and her body responded by gripping, then releasing from the burn.

"Good," Krampus said softly, forcing more and more of himself into her. "Take it. Take it all like a good girl."

The more cock she got, the wilder Lili felt. Krampus was so thick he was stretching her and the ginger made her feel like she had absolutely no control over her own body at all. She'd never felt anything like this; it was absolutely nothing at all like getting fucked by the local boys.

Who was this guy?

Krampus fucked her harder and faster, his claws digging in to the meat of her hips, pulling her back against him so she was taking his full length. Lili moaned into her apple and let him take her, allowing her body to shake and quiver around him. She had absolutely no control at all as the orgasm ripped through her. Her body seized up involuntarily and she didn't even care about the ginger's burn; in fact, it only increased her sensitivity.

Krampus held Lilibet still as her body convulsed around his. Once her orgasm died down he pulled his still hard cock out of her and pulled her to her knees in front of him.

"Get on your knees and suck me now," he commanded.

She didn't need to be told twice. She spit the apple from her mouth and took him deep into her throat, tasting her own juices on him. He grasped her hair and pushed himself deep into her mouth until she was gagging on him.

Lili used one hand to brace herself on his thigh and the other to stroke the length of him that she couldn't get into her mouth. It was the roughest blow job she'd ever given but she was melting like butter at Krampus' feet from that orgasm he'd just given her.

Lili could feel the cock harden in her mouth and she knew what was coming even before her mouth and throat filled with cum. She swallowed as much as she could, the remainder dripping from her lips onto the sweater still covering her breasts.

Krampus pulled himself from her mouth and tucked his cock back into his pants. He left her on the floor of the barn without so much as another word.

Lili pulled the ginger from her asshole and tossed it onto the compost, then rushed outside to catch him. She wanted to ask him his real name and she wanted to ask if she could see him again, but he was already gone.

There wasn't a trace of him.

She cleaned herself up a bit, made sure the animals had food, and headed back into the house.

"Lili!" her mother surprised her, sitting at the kitchen table. "You naughty girl, have you been out this whole time?"

Lili felt the color rush to her cheeks. There was no way that she could tell her mother what she'd been up to.

"Well," her mother gave her a sly grin, "just don't let your father find out. Keep your secrets. Go to bed, and next year maybe try to behave yourself so you don't end up on the naughty list again."

Lili gave her mother a suspicious look before heading up the stairs to bed, taking them two at a time, eager to get undressed and under the covers. She entered her room and shut the door behind her, stripping her clothes from her body and pulling on an old T-shirt and clean panties.

She pulled the comforter down on her bed ready to climb in and saw it... there, sitting on her pillow waiting for her was a chocolate orange.

* * *

B e the first to find out about all of Lee Riley's new releases, book sales, and freebies by joining her VIP Mailing List. Join today and get a FREE book -- instantly!

Check Lee Riley's website spicybestsellers.com for more books.

* * *

ABOUT LEE RILEY

* * *

Lee Riley is an adventurous writer who creates spicy short stories that challenge conventions and leave readers on the edge of their seats. Drawing inspiration from their travels, Lee explores the world with insatiable curiosity, using these experiences to craft stories that captivate readers.

When not writing, Lee indulges their passion for the outdoors, discovering new culinary delights, and making connections with people from all walks of life. Their love for adventure and zest for life is reflected in their work, which is daring, unconventional, and full of surprises.

More on www.spicybestsellers.com

Contact me at lee@spicybestsellers.com

* * *

Ingram Content Group UK Ltd.
Milton Keynes UK
UKHW021052140723
425136UK00014BA/369

9 781088 121306